Soraya Shalforoosh
This Version of Earth

Soraya Shalforoosh
This Version of Earth

Barrow Street Press
New York City

Designed by Robert Drummond
Cover illustration by Elke Claus
Author photo by Alberta Testanero

Published by Barrow Street Press
Distributed by:
     Barrow Street Books
     P.O. Box 1558
     Kingston, RI 02881

First Edition

Library of Congress Control Number: 2014951308

ISBN 978-0-9893296-3-7

CONTENTS

For my sister, Noelle, and in memory of our parents.
For my husband, Yanni, and son, Dylan.

SUBURBAN DINER

In black wool, silk, and rayon, rhinestones and fine perfumes,
Deirdre, Peter, and I eat omelets, lox, and sip milkshakes after
discothequing since midnight. The truck drivers watch us freaks eat.
We could be their kids, in another city, state, spending mall-earned
money, as we do, on dancing and a strange form of chic.

Wanda, our favorite waitress, with beehive and thicker polyester clothes
than we could dream of scoring at a Salvation Army, bats her false
eyelashes at us if we can't decide our orders fast enough, as if the joint
were ever packed.

In this newspaper-graying dawn, she's at the counter twirling the cake
tray and can't explain why lemon meringue pie is the cake special.
Go figure. She never does bat aneye at our tiaras, matching outfits,
or even when my sister does all three of our makeup the same.
Peter always the prettiest.

Later:

Watching Sunday papers being tossed onto neighbors' lawns as we exit
off Route 17 (one turn and I'm there). Dad's Cadillac might be out
front. He may haveentered our home's threshold (where an Islamic
prayer in black Farsi script wards offevil ghosts from entering) before
me, so I trace his tracks on the plush plum carpet. Or maybe his navy
Cadillac is not there yet.

Soon:

My cat will break into my room, smell Pepsodent off my teeth,
flop his tail into the warmth of my eyelet bed, my eyelet curtains
blinking to my clean God for the quiet of this home.
My ears still slightly humming, the sweat just off my body.

I am very good.

16 SONG

Fake IDs, new sneakers, shag rug faded blue:

Above my head tear-outs from *Vogue*, woman walking over rocks in a
    black fitted suit
Woman in sheer stockings graced on satin, half a breast exposed.
Siouxsie and the Banshees, *Juju*, sandalwood incense, Plimpton's *Edie*
    sifted through.
A short white go-go dress bought on Broadway for $16.00.
Gin bottles behind the bed.

I gave my phone number to a guy at a townie keg party; he's calling.

I feel stupid explaining I'm going to see The Jesus and Mary Chain
    tonight at the Ritz.
He's never heard of them. Of course not; he listens to Led Zeppelin.
So do I; it's in the tap water too, but I suddenly feel too NYC to
    somehow enjoy
Watching videos with a six-pack of beer and someone's arm around
    my neck
In a finished basement where someone will have a joint.

But, I can listen to noise until my ears rush through my feet
And dance until breakfast.

I'm perfectly asexual dodging glances from any man in the club
They have no clue I'm only 16 anyway.

Or do they?

I cling to my plastic cup of gin and tonic
I watch the fringe bang off my legs

My legs.
You know my hat is perfect, my lipstick too
Peter looks just like Morrissey
And I will wake up remembering dancing
Remembering, ah to be naked, 16, and perfectly alone.

NO NAME

WhEn I FiRst HeARd PunK
I feLt sAfe hAtiNg wAldWiCk
StuPid ToWn, pEOpLe

GOING OVER GOWANUS

That scowling dead man
In that oak coffin he's no
Help at all.

He's carried by three denim-clad hool-
igans. Fucking won't stop finger-whistling me.

I bury these beet-reddening cheeks into this over
cast wash sky.

There is no me reflected me under me in this trashed canal.

TEENAGE HEAVEN

Dark room; bong water
Pink snowballs; outside snowing
Love and Rockets; dream.

MAGIC

O silly girl
In the backyard by the forsythia bush
Did you ever know it would stop?

That your legs would be crossed and
Under Formica under flickering
Fluorescent bulbs making your complexion
Yellow as a buttercup?

That your fascination with wishing over weeds
Stars and pennies
Would be clumsily replaced, well not really
Replaced, but absorbed by paper?

Uh-huh. On this desk lurk stacks of paper
Black pencil, cup, stapler.

HOUSE WITH FILLING STATION

From sleep you shake me—
Gas for your empty yellow school bus.

In this pine forest, my house is the clearing.
I'd live alone here too, but I can't pump gas.

Ma'am the pumps are in the front yard.

No I can't explain how I can't pump gas
I just like its smell.

Won't you two bitches stop bickering
about why girls like me—
Stupid, or is it naïve, are so reliant.

Sweeping up after a thick pine crash
with a thick pine branch.
I am among the thickest of everything.

I AM THE STAR I WENT TO IRAN

I.

I brought to Iran a
Box of Toblerone chocolate almost as tall as I.
Farouj wanting chocolate wakes me: "Soraya be in ja."
I whisper in English: "*Where is my dad?*"
Oh, in a casino. Casino! Like Las Vegas or Monte Carlo.
Toss of chips; flick of red cards.
Green table, blue table, *soft*.
As an adult I am going to wear long scarves, fine perfumes, and spin
roulette wheels.
Farouj wants chocolate.
I have to open it; only I can.
Who else has an auntie waking her at 3 a.m. to eat chocolates?
Not anyone.
Oh, I am learning. It is only my second night here and I am learning.
We drink tea with sugar cubes in our teeth. This is what it must be like
to be a Queen!
I can sit on the floor even in the kitchen.
In open windows, there are cats, dogs; on floors salamanders,
cockroaches.
Somewhere close my dad has stacks of cash on a table, a cocktail on a
silver tray.

II.

11 a.m. and after
I awake; Dad's rubbing a warm cloth on my cheeks.
I got chocolate here? Oh, and on my pillow.

11 a.m. first time I slept past 7. I know from the way he laughs about
my being up with Farouj, that he won't tell mom ever.

He tells me he had too much to drink. But what does that even mean?
It means I
can eat chocolate.

Flying into Tehran was like flying into a Christmas tree with all its
lights. Here,
I walk on boxes and presents. If they are not for me, it doesn't matter;
they are.
Systematically somehow all the boxes, presents
Were wrapped into black wrap. What else would one want to see?
Everything that has ever been seen!

When I begin to tell what is hidden, you'll want more.
When you want more, we hide what's given.

FRESHMAN YEAR

Hey baby will you
Take me as your hostage? I
Can arrange it.

JUDGE BY BOOKS

I have read *Not With
Out My Daughter*. Was
It like that for *you*?

PASSED

Passed out while reading *Reading Lolita in Tehran*,
A highlighter snowflake on the duvet.
He unstuck my elevator; guess I looked like jailbait.
Why–is it so dark in here?
Moon sucked my vision, popping mad doses of vitamin A.
I'll flash my ankles to the passersby
Gotta love Larry; he's got a toolbox. Who wouldn't want it?
Not sure if I passed out or just saw The Light.
Breakfast tray, morning lay, a rose and a *New York Times*. Is she
enlightened? I'm melting into her head. Connection. We're all about
connecting and never understanding.
He roamed the streets, circled the block, over and
over. Something seemed familiar.

JUST GOT TO THE DECK

I am sweating, an anchor pull-
Ing. My psychic once nervously said:
I'd never get on a boat with you . . . sinking ships.

You've drowned before.

And I know that he is telling the truth.
My adolescent dreams of getting caught in a pond's beautiful
    green muck,
That sickening grip on the ankle.

Oh, he warned me.
Some life before it worked, wrecked.
My bones and dreams are karma's buried treasure.

The water, it wants you back.

Why did I do this? Small holiday adventure.

Pretend to ignore fear, as if that could save me.
Ridiculous! In my large black straw bag lurk
Sunscreen and a floppy hat.

All these people on this deck,
I may recklessly kill them
Just by my being

Here.

LIGHT AND THE MOONMAN

I have your wisdom mixed with mine.
Our silver lining is broken.
Even with your superhero umbrella, I am wet.
Our madness whimpers down the navy hallway, trippy passageway.

The drunken sandman sleeps in silt.
And the Moonman is up to his telepathy again.
My king, what a garden you have found.
We're in the tropics, we're in the desert, and we're in the backyard.
You're a rose dropping petals!
You're an egg bandit,
on this mischief's eve.

They say the cone off the pine, is mine.
This pine syrup drenched in dream dusk—
Then this heather-hued dawn

The sky is a trespasser.

THE JESUS AND MARY CHAIN

"Never understand"
Blasted year parents split up
Feedback over screams

CLASSIC ROCK LICK

Pathetic rush of adolescent shit beers we drank one night
flashes before me in smeared coats of mascara,
and boys I never thought—kissed anyway.   And it is all smeary and wet.
As the stupid guitars never stop soiling or soloing, slopping.
       I want to keep my future girls away from suburbs
we were wasting and repeating like this stupid lick. Lick.

HE WAS SINGING NUDE UP IN A TREE

He was singing nude up in a tree,
Belting out an opera concerto—he woke me
I had to walk to the end of the property
To find what had alarmed me. *Oh,*
Strange man up there in the oak tree
Singing so beautifully
Why are you naked, why in this dream? Why opera?
Why sing?
I don't even recognize you; I can't name this piece
Naked and you are neither fat nor slim
I can't even see your
   This limb causing a crucial obstruction
Why is it sky-blue out
If it is 3 a.m.?
Why startle me so?
Who lurks in my property?

Who lurks, whoa

MOM(S)

Professor asked
Me about life in Harem.
It was A plus, sir.

I SNEAKED INTO THE MOVIES THIS WEEKEND

It was my first time, and I'm 34. Why did it take so long?
Felt real fun. You see, the first film, which we paid for, was so sad and we had to cheer
ourselves up with some fluff. I loved the sneaking; so did my friend Suzanne.
But then I lost my leather gloves and the Lost and Found was closed.
That night, I dreamed about characters from the first film.
House of Sand and Fog. They were my friends.
Jennifer Connelly likes to scuba dive and listens to Sheryl Crow. I sent Ben Kingsley my résumé, and became his personal assistant.
I even made him eggs, sunny-side up, while he smiled at me.

I didn't dream the lost house, the son killed, the suicides. Weird, eh? You see, like
Kingsley's character I am Iranian-American, and his daughter's name is *Soraya.* She
had only a small role. But it was the first time I heard my name in the cinema, I think.
And, like the Connelly character, my child house is lost, taken by auction.
So, why didn't I dream *these* things? Why didn't I dream parallels?

I didn't dream the sneaked-into film: *Mona Lisa Smile* with Julia Roberts. I didn't
dream undergraduate days in Massachusetts, which I did do, too. And, I didn't even
dream Giselle, the student having the affair(s), disappointed and seeking sex, the one
whose parents are divorced, the one going to get hurt. I didn't dream that, no.

YOU CAN'T STAND IT WITHOUT ME

I know because I can hear you
       Screaming my name at night.
I hear you screaming 10,000 miles away.

I've leaped into your dreams
I can tell you that your dream
Of that boat sinking in the Thames
       Means that you miss me.
It means you miss me
When you smack your mattress
       Smack your cold hard mattress hard after your fingers
Have hunted for my shape, my big breasts, hips you love.

I left you tossing
       On white-and-yellow checked sheets
Tossing to an infinity of no-more-sleeping nights

I can feel, taste, see my name
Escaping out your mouth like fists
Tiny punches to the cold silent air

I know I am this air.

LOOSE CHANGE

Who is walking those rooms?
Stepping where I have.
She barely sits on his sofa.
Who is she?
My God, she's got such little presence, so little to say,
and what she does say is stupid.
Do you think she can even feel me?
Tugging her hair,
pulling the slubs on her silk blouse?
I stain her eyes, silly sloppy rings of mascara.
I appear, ghost of a girl,
girl who touched him before she did
I appear in both their dreams:
I'm here, I'm here
dancing big, singing so loud so
that her little frame shakes.
Shaking into the couch
she slips into the cracks of the couch.
He can't save her.

I'LL NEVER FORGET THE TIME HE SMASHED IN HIS OLD BOSS'S CAR

An old boss who never paid him.
He smashed it in with his golf club.
I just watched as the once-smooth blue car was clubbed
to broken glass, dented tin.
I was mesmerized by my boyfriend's ability to destroy.
His body turned to thick bulging brute biceps
A chin pointing like an attacking dagger. He crippled
That car. His face so red
His head full of sweat
When he stopped.

He came over to me in our car, smiling. He swooped down
Kissed me on the forehead
"We better hurry." He put the key in the ignition,
His other hand on my soft leg,
Calming him.

BONES OVER BONES

I
toss a bone
from a drunken 1 a.m. urge for
chicken tandoori into the cemetery.

Bones over bones.

My boyfriend is pissing into the bush behind me.
His pissed drunken friends swaying ahead tell me to "hurry up,
don't wait for him!" I suck the last bone,

toss it so far so fast
it lands on a gravestone
that I bet no one has ever hit with a chicken bone before.

NEW YORK WOMAN (I HAVE ALLERGIC REACTIONS TO ALUMINUM)

Thought it was just teen hatred of everything
that made me hate suburbs and hive at aluminum siding.
But I still hate aluminum siding, strip malls, and I spend
more annually on thongs and vodka
than my mom did on groceries for a family of four.
Well, I never set out to be *this*.
It happens, *New York woman*. It seems dangerous to give it up.
I know there are serious consequences to having a backyard.
A house, a driveway, these people you must come home to.

WARLOCK

My dream catcher is failing
Bad taste of nightmare and
Oh god, slippers in the dark.
Too much sex so I'm stuck reading the thesaurus
What, no entry for warlock or witch? *Crazy book.*
I have three spells to discuss highness.
I am the highness, who is the highness?
Send some sand. Send his kiss
Go forward kiss my ring now
This is the land to build your moat around
Like a boa slipping off my neck
I will keep you here
In here
Awake

OVER OUR LIGHTNING

You hibernate, O, how you're night-designed.
Ah, in my sick toiling, reverent rolling
You are silent, creeping on clouds. A hint:

Our heroes are aghast! What a host, your
Horizons have slammed shut. Bow! Our
Absurdity of feelings under zealous

Believing. Future: yet another night to lie down.

Oh, I'm sick under our good moon. Our good man,

I refuse to die bowing! Oh, but I am vexed, maybe from
Insufficient bowing? I swear longest hour
Truth sick night! After you lift off, after red dice roam

Reciting the numbers, seven at home.

DREAM AT THE MIDDLE OF THE YEAR

All the Indian restaurants were in luxury high rises.

The ubiquitous pink elephant smoked a hookah. I had to pull you
out of the Sunshine Curry to tell you, "I won the jackpot at the Feast of
St. Anthony raffle!"

You smelled of cherry-infused tobacco and Taj Mahal lager.

Walking over "Page Six" bums to just get to the other end of sleep,
         there I found
                          I was the towering Buddha with a bird's-eye view of
$20,000 dollar boobs, $16 ginger-infused cocktails shaken and poured into
chilled martini glasses.

What happened, Manhattan?

WORK POEM

I'm a tired six of spades
Open window, city is a loud fuzz, I am blocked by a Dell
As I watch shy people make smaller talk
Work life after work life.
Midtown, downtown, loft space
I'm still in the bungalow of rich man's new clothes
Fabrications of the new century
Modern Zen hipsters unshiny in the white orchid reflection

POEM PLANT

Take clouds cats cotton
Swirls some simmer sun sexed
Have poem: two (w̶)days.

WEEK AFTER 9/11

My coworker asks
Why are all the falafel
Shops closed? Did they know?

NOWRUZ

You brought apples, sumac, *sabzeh*, garlic, and a little vinegar—
What was she cooking? the others wondered.

Another day, coins, and hyacinth plant. Then, the mirror
from your vanity and your Polish painted wooden eggs, assembled on
the table next to your desk. A mystery to those peering into your office.
She must be a witch.

Yes, for days, you brought in what you could in your tote bag.
What wouldn't leak or break on your drive up the mountains, then
as you hobbled on your arthritic legs to the (prison school), your
regulated office. You had to make a *Haft-Seen* for your one Persian pupil.
Nowruz in confinement.

The California Youth Authority never saw a celebration like this,
hidden in the pale - green walls, you, Mom, a 60-year-old rule breaker.

Smuggling in the sweet, the bitter
Elements of the Eternal.

DARK MOON

Mom, I walked to work and saw this waning crescent moon disappearing
into the wee hours of the sky.
Simultaneously in my mind I was wondering where you *really are*
Then—
On the cobblestone street the equation hit, MOM

You are the new moon.

The dark moon.

My heel stuck into a crack of pothole on Wooster Street, as I was struck
Then smiled, no one but you

OCEAN

Mom. When I think of you I usually think of the stars, sky, that you're "out there" somewhere. And this week when drifting to sleep, I thought of the ocean instead, that I would meet you,
again in the ocean tides, that we would rise up and down together, sunlight would shine over us, whether we are amoebas, or fish darting through coral, maybe dolphins? That we would be splashing, or maybe in splashes, or splashes themselves—maybe we'd be the Ocean and embrace all limbs with a foam that sticks, a foam that kisses sand, seashells that are picked over by birds and maybe the sound of little pink shells rattling on the surf is your call.

It is raining on this version of earth; I accidentally stepped into a sooty puddle.

I'll take what I can get.

UNCLE ALI DIED ON JULY 19TH, 2005

The day Uncle Ali died of natural causes in a hospital in Tehran, Iran,
A storm hit Northern NJ with such ferocity that lightning burned a
gash into his nephew's home—ash and debris clouded the living room.

The bizarre mix of Persian and suburban domesticity mangled inside a
warped diorama: the deep hole in the aluminum-sided house revealed a
burnt Persian rug, a dust-drenched samovar, and my cousin Victoria
only a foot away, watching TV.

Uncle Ali's shock therapy in Switzerland during the '60s didn't work.
His final 30 years were spent in an institution in his hometown of
Tehran. Outside his institution windows another bloody revolution,
another bomb dropped, and another.

Outside the windows it was mostly black. But there was a time for Ali
at the Caspian Sea, voices of sunshine meeting rock and fresh grilled
meats nearby, clouds to watch drift toward Russia. And once a time of
being a student far away in America.

Moving to Washington D. C. with my father, Ali Asghar.
Learning English with Ali Asghar, going to Clemson, studying
engineering, and then it just isn't clear. A hole, a gash, a space,
Uncle Ali.

MOTHER'S DAY DRINKS

Mother's Day brunch was not a brunch; we went when only the bar
        was open.
Sat outside on a gorgeous May 13th 70° day
And drank caipirinhas on the corner of Avenue C and 9th Street.
A dark box of a bar and it was a bright day. And we watched
heroin addicts barely make their steps down the block, plop on the sidewalk
        and prepare for another shot.
We watched a pack of young men on bicycles, the coked-up waitress
explain the kitchen was closed over and over,
the blondest family who seemed the same color as the sun walk to the park
        in amazement.
Then the blue, green, and red enamel earrings from my husband and cat.

SHARK

It was so painful those sharks biting my leg
And the shark attack wasn't mine; it belonged to my dead mother
And in the middle of the bloody ocean
The shark bites turned to small puncture wounds in my feet
And I appeared at a doctor's office
And I could walk
And I was on land—dry
It was so bright and my eyes had to adjust
And I was explaining
On a beige velvet couch.

MERCURY RETROGRADE

I just got to Newark when they announced my flight to Chicago was
  Canceled.

I said "Fuck you!" when I meant to say, "Excuse me, please."

A drunk nun walked right into me and scowled.

I sent the e-mail for my headhunter to my boss; shoot.

I screamed my cat's name during sex.

I fell up the hill.

I ran into an old lover and looked like shit.

The ATM ate my bank card jamming the machine and the line behind
  me angry.

The power went out when the dentist had the drill in my tooth.

He exclaimed, "Your pussies are so big and your breast so tight!"

My cat chewed through the phone cord and my cell battery died.

That guy with the top hat is sending loud telepathic messages that he
  hates me.

There are major delays in the Holland Tunnel. Will I ever get to the air-
  port on time?

NAKED BILLBOARDS IN TIMES SQUARE

Woe is me city, the billboards are empty!

They can't seem to rent out the $20,000 spots in our troubled economy. Woe, Times Square, of seedy stripper booths then transformed to a Giuliani Disney playground, and now you're pedestrian-friendly by Bloomberg, your transformations, your utility.

The free MTA bus ride the weekend of the blackout from the Upper West Side to SoHo, how patches of city were without lights, so surreal to see Times Square black. And, in the yonder of where the grid would pop back up, lights!

O, Times Square of Tad's Steaks House, where my cousin once threw up. I was 12. I was petrified. He drank 6 martinis.

O, Times Square of my life as an event planner, in chain hotels with tacky bad carpet in their banquet rooms, the neon-signed piano bars with salty snacks.

O, Times Square of my first job, the bus commute home to and from northern NJ to Port Authority. It was 1991, and the heroin addicts and crackheads lined my walk to the 7 train. The mariachi bands serenading us, the mystery liquid that seeped through cracks in the endless tunnels. The shuttle to Grand Central, the break dancers who resembled popcorn in an electric popper, each limb electrifying.

O, Times Square of Greyhound and Peter Pan buses to and from Massachusetts. O, the college commutes to school. Praying I'd make it without a trip to the turbulent loo. I would listen to Love and Rockets, or Echo & the Bunnymen, over and over, the sound track of I-95. Smartfood and CD player, I was armed for you.

O, Times Square of prostitutes in latex and spandex dresses not sure of the sex, but man that is some dress. And feeling a cold sore rise just by looking.

O, Times Square your Calvin Klein skinny Kate, cocaine Kate, model ads. With your pre-puberty sex kittens, remember Brooke? Nothing came between her and her Calvins. O, Times Square, I read in the current market woes that your billboards are
naked.

SWING

Lynne will not contribute to the office Lotto pool
She needs to save her singles for strippers
At Meow Mix. Or she is the one, mad dancing on the weekends,
After a few mojitos in bad heels dancing to Cuban music
But. . .

On weekdays, she faces Marlene.
Ms. Dietrich pasted all over her cubicle, and, did
I tell you that this is an investment bank? A quiet
Conservative one in Midtown, with views of everything. The celebrity
Bisexual stunning with cigarette holder staring at all of us who pass,
Seems marvelously out of place. And,

As the traders swing their invisible golf clubs
Getting geared up for Friday on the green

On the floor I am, hearing them all wish for a hole in one.

FLUID

Quick cocktails after work
Then went to yoga
Not enlightened
Fell
            Asleep in serpent's pose
My hot face drooling on the mat

Sounds of feet woke me
They moved on.

EXERCISE CLASS

I had to curl my legs into my chest, my head up, chin tucked.
I had to rock back and forth. And I am not a daffodil
I am not a jonquil or iris, just a very ordinary human
Who has been hanging inside a lantern.
She said *scoop scoop scoop from your abdomen*
My shoulder blades cracked an invisible walnut; I was a seal, a swan.
I tell myself I am not a flower, just a silly human who likes to watch
        goldfish at the pond.
My muscles are bending wrong; they could move more efficiently.
What do you do for a living?
I work at a day job, and I'm a poet, I said.
Huh, she said.
I don't know how else to make money, I said.
But now my muscles move wrong. My petals shake to the floor at night.
Inside the bed I Am—and my stamen is detached staring at me from the
ceiling. Rock back inside Yourself.
What do you do for a living? I'm just a silly human. I am not a painting,
or a flower. I Have lost my ears; I have a tongue in my sleeve. My senses
are long-winded. My Abdomen
Will scoop someday.

PSYCHICS ARE THRIVING

The dynamics have changed, maybe bad feng shui?
The fresh-faced Vassar girl is already bitter
What has finance done to us? Our souls leaking in the hallways,
        entranceways
All over this city hedge funds are vomiting
And the networking network sites are out of bounds
NY Metro says, "Psychics are thriving." One tony Upper East Side
astrologer limits visits From the Unemployed clients, so not to be a
career coach. What a star.

This glorious spring fizzled into flannel, gray and wet; it is so London
for NYC. *Where is Hugh Grant?* The red cheeks, the despair, SoHo is
all 60% off.
But I still see Paris Hilton wannabes. What gives?
Poetry and sex are still free. Sex they say is on the (ahem) rise, and
poems spurt up like Crocuses out of splits in sidewalks.

SOMEWHERE ON 19TH STREET LAMA NORLHA
IS AND ISN'T

Jay says Lama Norlha is everywhere

He is many irises. He is the 100 eyes across this room. He
has red carpet in his bedroom, blue carpet in the living room. *He
eats meat. You see in Tibet, Buddhists eat meat.* I don't eat red meat,
but I eat chicken and fish. *Lama Norlha can look right at you, and he
knows what you are thinking.* I said, scary. *Lama Norlha is here from
Tibet to help us; he is compassionate, not insulting,* Jay says.

I repeat scary. You see I'm scared that Lama Norlha will
look at me then see I am thinking helpless that I am thinking
something sad or very stupid and he will fill up my head or my
rib cage and when I breathe he'll know that I breathe bad; he will
see my air, my head, and he will cry too. But I don't want to make
Lama Norlha cry. And if he hugs me then just tell me which ribcage
is mine, which rib cage is his? Tell me which is the ceiling, which
the sunrise? If you look at me from your eyes across our rooms

If you look at me what will?

UPRIGHT

The entire subway ride
His face with goatee peeping out behind her neck
And how he held her hand on her L o n g c u r v e s casual yet firm.
Oh, how it looked so warm. When the train stopped at 2nd Avenue (both
      our stops)
he swept her up off the ground and held her even tighter.
She, so heavy, more than me, than you. He carried her with grace, elegance.
No one would push into her, bang into her with bags, just up and
over the turnstile, up two flights of steps into night air   I followed them
      panting, he a
steady stream of breath. Then he put her back down.
Rolled her up 2nd Avenue.

It is four blocks after I depart the two. I know that somewhere tonight in
      this city she is
everything I want to b.   She
Larger than life so deeply sensual oh yes, she is
The crux and buzz of a smoky club she is. How she will stand in his arms
He who makes her resound so that hundreds of listeners will be nodding. I
      have heard it
seen it, felt it myself! Not him, her.
Smacking their hands onto their tables, their laps, moaning for his fingers to
keep going to keep working over her like this, like that.

SOHO BRIDE

SoHo bride thought the closing of 2006 was ridiculous
with that celebration of a hanging.
It's New Year's death squad, not a baby.
Did anyone know it was Eid al-Adha?
2006 was also the year of overwaxed celebrity private parts getting headlines.
Waxed crotches flashed for paparazzi, while sliding in and out of sports cars.
I have so much wedding planning to do. I hope tomorrow is not a disaster.
There are velveteen bunnies in my future. Some double-breasted suits are
cheesy.
How am I supposed to write a poem when my head is everywhere?
SoHo bride is using a trainer. I am doing sumo squats with a 30-lb dumbbell
behind my head. Man, I hate pull-ups. SoHo bride is scheduling and
unscheduling appointments: eyebrow maintenance, dress fittings, and I'm on
Weight Watchers. . . and I can't stop snacking. How did I start this poem?
Oh yes, death!
Instead of a New Year's baby we get New Year's death squad.
The cycle will repeat itself. Tell me, how will death bring peace?
How will our enemies ever forgive us?
Scraggly *New York Times* reporters are angry and tired; they seem irate at
the dumb questions from the newscasters in cozy warm studios. Come on!
These guys are in the field risking their lives for information that our media
ignores or distorts. "Iraqis have to take responsibility."
Excuse me, last time I checked we bombed the fuck out of their country;
last time I checked we killed their children, raped their women, and lit
their families on fire.
Iraqi responsibility. . . Paris Hilton should get an ISBN on her crotch,
and as soon as I thought this I realized I meant to write *bar code*.
My head really hurts; my head needs a filter.
Soon I will get married, and still be Soraya Shalforoosh.
My sunshine hurts.
These dreams within these dreams with biting wizards, lackluster
honeymoon phobia.

I'm so scared of getting bit by malaria-infected mosquitoes, and
I'm even more scared to take the tabs to ward that off. I want eggs
and seashells.
I want a new Pilates instructor, hamstring stretching to the ceiling.
Oh no! A cockroach on the floor. My nails are Parisian Tango. Red
red, red sunrise, my sky loves your red is a jaguar red as her lingerie
red as my lucky suit.
I haven't been sleeping much.
I wish I owned a dust ruffle so I could just hide the good wine and
porn. I ate way too many pistachios. My head has gone unordered.
I would like to retrace my steps to see.

Somewhere vicious I fell asleep.

"MOVE ON FAST"
(title of a song by Yoko Ono)

My messenger
Our Ouija
Vivacious voice
Excuse, enchanting

O, October and November souls

First nervous, *Ghost*
Alarming, answer
Spell spirits,
Tell me.

DAD WAS HOME FOR WEEKS RECOVERING

Sitting in the recliner, you seemed so much smaller, watching game
shows with spinning wheels and jumping moms with bad perms. You
agreed to be Charlie as in *Charlie's Angels* as we ran around the rooms.
I was Sabrina, of course. Kim was Kelly. With our walkie-talkies and
imaginary guns we were going after a bad guy.

Was it 1979 or 1980 when two men held you upside down in a bar
while the third punched. "Fucking Iranian." Broken ribs, broken
everything but spirit. How did you do it Dad? Not get bitter?

DAD LOVED THE SONG "DUST IN THE WIND" BY KANSAS

And it was annoying that it played in my head as I sat in the ICU waiting room. I thought of it on the 8 track, the fake wood console, or playing as he drove his Cadillac with automatic windows. Though Dad listened mostly to Persian disco, the occasional western song entered his repertoire. Kansas "Dust in the Wind" or Pat Benatar "I'm Gonnato Follow You"

Now Dad is somewhere I hope dancing crazy. As he made the car dance, the house shake. His photo on a prayer card following me through every room in the house now.

Tomorrow is Ash Wednesday, and ash and dust on the heads and minds of many.
We are all going to die, I know.

I know we are going to stare at the crocus shoots through the grass and say, "It's an early spring" as we eat eggs and think about renewal.

In 40 days, I will paint those eggs with my son. I don't even know why we celebrate Easter, but we did and do. The chocolate bunnies, and *babka*. Easter is sweet and colorful.

Dad, I don't know what you're doing anywhere. But you are so much more than Dust.

FLOATING

my father is alive
he is driving a car
in Cape Cod, he is driving the twisty roads of the Caspian
he is driving 60, 70, dare he—yes 85 hoping not to get caught
we are almost tasting waves
we are near where mom is
they are in sand dunes now
they have hot sand burning their feet
they are lifting me up by the arms and swinging me
they are washing my bucket of shells
in the sea foam
the foam is stuck in my hair
I stood on the beach and watched them float
away

come back! I screamed little girl running up and
down the shores of the Caspian, "Mom don't go to Russia, you can't come back"
Daddy laughing
Noelle found a snake under a rock
I am running up and down the shore
"Mom come back!"

Don't float that way

APPEAR

Pictures of parents on funeral cards
Following me from bedroom to car seat
My third eye is thumping
A seahorse appears on the sidewalk
Today the taste of pistachios
I hear a constant thunder of rolling backgammon dice
The shaking exploding in my legs
Dad is big as a ghost in my new office
He sits by the window like a cat in sun
And then tells me to tell them all to ***** off
Mom wants me to become a teacher
I am trying to think about a religion class
My son asked me if Jesus rose from the dead
How come Grandpa didn't
Last night I bought a new home by the sea
Big open windows dark water
Out the living room all the pet owls sat on a bar
They were so snuggly and cute all of them white and black with the big
soulful eyes from watching the woods at night
But aha, they were in my new home
My son found a purple feather at the restaurant
He tried to give it to the hostess who didn't seem to appreciate his magic
Amazing for me, but I did not say a word just
Watched him wave his wand

DEATH

Autopilot has stopped, that coffee won't work.
Five trees in Shasta Park planted in his memory from my colleagues.
That was more than four months ago.
Do they know I am still somewhere between the sounds he emitted
post-tubes-removal and the plane landing in California to escape?
The Pacific highway is therapy. I witnessed the windy road.
Drove through that famous Leggett tree.
On the way there we saw gorgeous coast, tallest trees, and vultures
eating fresh kill. Their large stomachs spectacular and black, their beaks
in conjunction not competition. Death works that way.
And I tasted the wines of Mendocino County, Anderson Valley, and,
yes, Napa.
I was flat on a massage table in a swank hotel.
My best friend Rachael who took me away to recover from your death,
Dad. *You remember her, my roommate from Scotland, my bridesmaid.*
sigh

We are that sad club, our parents are all dying.
Her dad dead too.
But Mom, and you too Dad,
lost to separate car accidents—seems impossible.
The huge personalities, can they both be contained in heaven?
Are they listening to my thoughts?
Or are they part of my brain now?
I have no religion but Earth!
Ah, sea foam and metaphor, my goddesses.

I missed the tunnel entrance, I missed the meeting, the e-mail, the
door, forgot my keys, my money, I overspent, I am stingy, I returned to
the gym, went to every doctor, laughed inappropriately, was scared to
sleep, was scared to let go of my husband,
my son's hand, my mom's purple comb, the sound of my dad dying.
His face looked as if it was about to smile. He looked like a smile. A
happy man surrounded by faces watching for his last breath. Then it
happened—

and Hamid almost collapsed. I waited till everyone left and kissed him
again and again. If my husband weren't there I'd be on the hospital floor,
still.

But I managed to get out of that room with him.

I managed to get to April, WAIT, this is now the first of July.

I managed to somehow get here and in front of you, computer.

My conscience is pounding at the top of my head

I am just a breathing blob.

MEASURING WITH DAD

My father is measuring rooms, clipboard in his hand.
Tape measure, pen. He is measuring their rooms for wall-to-wall
plush carpet.
I step on the tape for him; it's my job. I am seven and I have a job
It makes all the customers laugh. I know how important it is for the
tape measure to be straight. I get to ride in the truck. We get our
breakfast at a diner with the mechanic named Lefty. No traffic on
Route 17 this early.

Sunday, at the warehouse, I jump on mountains of rolls of padding.
My first and only skateboard is a dolly. I ride all over dreaming of being
bigger and out of this warehouse.
But I want to spend time with my dad. It's his day off when our store
is closed.

ACKNOWLEDGMENTS

Poems from this volume appeared previously (sometimes in somewhat different form) in the following places:

"New York Woman (I have allergic reactions to aluminum siding), "Mercury Retrograde," *American Poet*, Academy of American Poets

"Freshman Year," "Judge by Books," "Passed," "Mom(s)," "Dream at the Middle of the Year," "Work Poem," "Week after 9/11," "Dark Moon," "Shark," "Naked Billboards in Times Square," *Barrow Street*

"16 Song," *Can We Have Our Ball Back*

"Somewhere on 19th Street Lama Norlha Is and Isn't," *Crux and Brink: An Anthology of Post Modern American Poetry*

"Exercise Class," *Good Foot*

"I Am the Star I Went to Iran," *Iranian.com*

"Just Got to the Deck," *Lumina*

"Magic," *Marlboro Review*

"I Sneaked into the Movies this Weekend," *MiPOesias*

"Light and the Moonman," *Octopus*

"You Can't Stand it without Me," *Salonika*

"Going over Gowanus," "He Was Singing Nude up in a Tree," "Over Our Lightning," *Skanky Possum*

"Dad Was Home for Weeks Recovering," "Measuring with Dad," *Taos Journal*

"Bones over Bones," *Unpleasant Event Schedule*

"Uncle Ali Died on July 19th, 2005," *Women's Studies Quarterly*

My deepest gratitude goes out to the following individuals who over the years offered endless support: Jeffery Conway, Gillian McCain, Martha Rhodes, Patricia Spears Jones, Daisy Wake, Susan Wheeler, David Trinidad, Robert Polito, David Lehman, Kathleen Krause, Rebecca Reilly, Kathleen Ossip, Mark Bibbins. And I can never give thanks enough to Melissa Hotchkiss, Peter Covino, Sarah Kruse, and everyone at *Barrow Street*. A big thanks and smooch to my husband, Yanni, and our son, Dylan, for their patience with me while I turned family vacations into poetry workshops and worked on poems at strange hours.

BARROW STREET POETRY

This Version of Earth
Soraya Shalforoosh (2014)

Unions
Alfred Corn (2014)

O, Heart
Claudia Keelan (2014)

Last Psalm at Sea Level
Meg Day (2014)

Vestigial
Page Hill Starzinger (2013)

You Have To Laugh: New + Selected Poems
Mairéad Byrne (2013)

Wreck Me
Sally Ball (2013)

Blight, Blight, Blight, Ray of Hope
Frank Montesonti (2012)

Self-evident
Scott Hightower (2012)

Emblem
Richard Hoffman (2011)

Mechanical Fireflies
Doug Ramspeck (2011)

Warranty in Zulu
Matthew Gavin Frank (2010)